An American Papyrus

WITHDRAWN

POEMS BY
STEVEN DAVID JUSTIN SILLS

CHESTNUT HILLS PRESS
MCMXC

Acknowledgements

"The Politics of Herb's Woman" was published in *New Mexico Humanities Review.* "Man of Coal" was published in *Samisdat.*

To Mike Burns,

*poet and professor at Southwest Missouri State University,
I wish to express the highest degree of gratitude for his
altruistic dedication of time and energy to make the
editorial comments, over myriad years, that have resulted
in the refinement of this work. His contributions cannot be
underestimated, and this response is only a shallow
acknowledgment of the gratitude that I feel.*

CONTENTS

AN AMERICAN PAPYRUS

Afferent, the city bus cramps to the curb and brakes through
Solipsistic muteness with an exhaltation startled and choking.
As the sun blazes upon the terminal's
Scraped concrete
The shelved rows of the poor men
Hear the sound die on the pavement
In a gradual dying echo.
A cigarette succumbs to the voice as
Carrion brought to life; all the tattered people awaken;
And a man spits toward the tire of the bus,
But misses.

And as he watches his own spit vanish
From the hard crest of the world,
And silently scrapes his lunch pail against
A corner of a metallic bench as if expecting the pale to bleed . . .
And hoping it would bleed . . . he tries to remember the angles
He and his wife stood to project
The intermingled shadows that both
Had labeled as their marriage.

He enters the second bus:
Its coolness sedating the skin that
Overlaps his troubled mind.
His thoughts pull together
Like the light, cool flow of the air conditioning.
He feels a little pacified.
He knows the shadow's intangible depth:
Its vastness having overpowered him these months
Until he could not reach the logic that told him
To find himself outside its barriers.
As he stares out of the window
He wonders why she has left.
How could she have left without indication
When he has remained angled toward work

So that he and his wife can stay alive?
In the bus window he sees his diaphanous face — the windows
Of the Hilton, where he has a job in maintenance,
Piercing solidly through its head. He rings the bell.
The idea of her not home, and legally annulled
From his life — her small crotch not tightened to his desperate
Thrusts — makes him feel sick. He gets down from the bus.
He goes to work. He suddenly knows that he is not in love.

I use her earth to plant my seed —
My limbs twisting around the collective molecules,
Trying to dig in.
Only the obscurity of my body
Presses so fully that it is neither
Body nor bed nor the intersection of both,
But euphoric traction; and then, planted and repulsed,
Only the seam of backbone minutely faces her,
That bed of earth. With all conscious force
I breathe the aloneness that untangibly defines the
Air. I swallow its ambrosia
Of depth and ask myself why I ever
Married the woman. There is void.
Then a hollow answer calls my name and says "it was time."
I realize myself in movement, parting the scene.

I use what has been planted for the reaping —
My suit tucks me into its structure of cotton;
And soon a building will be again the structure
Around men of cotton suits, pushing a product.

Lost, I drink my coffee alone on the stoop.
She had asked to fix me breakfast
But I would not let her. My miniature is one
And black. I drink me in when I am not
Pressed by the coffee's steam.
Cars' casketed phantoms of people
Chasing up and down Dunlavy Street of Houston
After something — their whole lives after something —
Come and go from consciousness like respiration.
The people plant and reap, Who can count all of their
Insignificant names? —
Animals that are not created sensible enough
To propagate unless lost to frenzy,
Caught in structures without meaning.

We Mongoled human experience. We pushed it into our
    mouths
As the crisp pretzels of which the shape became salty dust at
Our tastes: the crispness of life,
And we Mongoled human experience.

The tequila, that Sandras or Cassandras, or whomever it had
Been at the moment of malevolently blessing our heated and
Maddening consumption, was what we left
Our wives for; and then hardened ourselves on
The springless cushions of the sofas of our friends
Whom we eventually forgot the names of: the wetness of human
Experience that we Mongoled, and felt the bladed emptiness
Of stomachs that could not consume food
On mornings after. But the Angels of bar rooms continually
Appeared before darkened stages where, in front of guitars, we
Played. They appeared at various stages to the weeks of the
Years. They came, silently whispering themselves off
As Sandras or Cassandras; stared up at us
For two hours; and disappeared.
The reappearance of their light enamored us, and we left
And followed but found bats that offered
No shelter, and often caves we could not fit into or were
Forbidden from entering.

We invested our capital
In the Silicon Valleys of this great nation.
Third-world bitches, in factories, became sick for our chips.
We held power.
We bred metals and bought the ownership titles
Of properties, but could not find a home of the world.
We married again and brought forth children
Whom were duplicate strangers of ourselves.

THE RETARDED

Legs clamp around the rim —
The whole seated body sticking slightly
As moaning howls come from his
Paralyzed mouth. It is after
having put him to bed for a nap, and then the pot,
That this woman who would dab the bile
From his bed like one who napkins a spill from
A tablecloth, does not clean away
The substance behind the smell
Which predominates over the bathroom urinal
And aggravates his senses.
No woman to do these tasks,
And then to rim her hand
Under the butt;
No woman to drag him from
The pot,
After she has had his body bent
Toward her for the wiping,
And flop him onto the bench
In the shower; no woman . . .

She sits, cigarette limp in her mouth,
Thinking that this day has almost ended.
And the stars she stares out at
From the living room of the group home
She remembers are other earths limping
Half-free in the grips of other
Dying suns.

HOUSTON

In Houston's summers the gods
Use the clouds as urinals
For three minutes daily.
In Houston the Boat-people
Come from planes.

Inner-city — intermingled and alone
Like its green Buffalo-Bayou
Strewn only in the imaginations
Of those who run along it briefly.

A mile from the bayou
The settled imagination of a
Nine year-old Vietnamese girl
Allows a mangled brown horse
To elongate and flatten out
To the reality of the rolled up carpet
(All because of the rain).
She feels the wetness now beginning
To seep into her clothes;
She raises herself; she sees the old Cuban
Walking from the house with hands
To the sky, as if to make the heavens appear a little longer
In the manner that the downtown buildings,
From Dallas Street on, by their
Stories of windows draw down
The sky's enormity from measurement
Both extensive and inadequate;
And she follows him.

Apart
And yet they both think about the Vietnamese
Teenager with curlers in her hair
Who yells "boo" behind doors
That are entered;

The Cambodian boy who
To the view of the Montrose area
Pours on the bare shrubs,
And then strips and pours upon himself,
The water from a hose, and that both animal and plant
Glisten in the sun
As if they have been greased;
Falling into Houston's world of high buildings
From the descending planes
While hoping that the big world would
Not overpower their memories;
And the Cubans, in house #2 always yelling of "Miami."
They believe that Cambodian refugees
Always clean house #1,
That Africans never clean themselves,
And that Laotians often pour rice down the drains
Causing the faucets of the house to stop-up;
And that the Welcome-center Manager
Does not care to bring over a little clothing
And a little food or take them on little trips
To the Social Security Office or the doctor's office
Past 5 p.m. —
But of different seconds in that minute,
Different lengths, and various perceptions.
She remembers the ugly man
In Vietnam that ran from the police
And then a scar around his eye
Opened from the clubs and the blood
Tried to escape him completely
As the body attempted to pull itself
From the street, and could not.
He remembers thinking that the
Cranium of an old man is always heavy
On the neck, and that his
Is becoming like this.

He desires to clasp the gate
That is around the Hispanic cemetery
And watch the cars on Allen Parkway, below,
Curve and toward the sun
Become a gleam moving endlessly
And instantly gone.
He desires to arrive there and
Read a few tombstones
Before and after watching.
She desires to imagine horses
Carrying her away from here to the West,
And other horses following with her family behind.
She desires to follow the Cuban that she fears
Since he is moving away from the refugee houses.
There are no horses in inner-city; and
The Hispanic cemetery cannot be found
To souls wanting to rest there.
"Este cerca de calle Alabama?"
He wonders.

The rain stops. The hammers and saws
Peel their sounds from a roof.
And he notices her steps,
Despite the stronger sounds; halts;
And glances behind him as shingles fall ahead,
While wanting her to completely leave him
And wanting her to come with him.

In Houston's summers,
At certain areas, shingles like
The gods' shit fall from housetops
And the dung dries in the air,
Flattens, and ricochets to sidewalks.
In Houston Cubans pack
From refugee houses

And plan to fly away into America, and depart
Far from the Castilian hot-dog vender
Of Herman Park waiting for
The thirsty and hungered
And those ignorant of what they want
But know that they want something
And so come to buy from her
Who wants people to come to her
For more than the chips
Because the hotdogs are overpriced,
Who formulates
That she is unskilled
And that a computer course would answer it all;
Far from the Netherland psychologist who
Stares at her ebony reflection
In Rothko Chapel's dyed pool;
Apart from others, and no-one, all
Pulling alone for humanity to both
Come and go from their lives.

THE POLITICS OF HERB'S WOMAN

Waitresses lightly frisbeeing out
Dishes of breakfasts
Catching glimpses of Colonel North's
Photos on the front sides
Of customers' papers and
Formulating judgments
Of rebel or martyr
From an appearance
And a few words that
Drifted in when the
Hands relaxed plates to table mats;
Farmers wishing the seeds
To suddenly open to be plucked up faster
So that they are not
The last ones laid in
By their hands;
Little "third-world" nations of people hoping
For the great debtor nation to continental-drift
To bankruptcy, painless and alone;

And nearly empty of thoughts — Herb's woman, Jeanie,
Behind the Ellison Building standing
With concrete drilling its stiffness
Through her soles.
There had been a time —
With face raised from her age-smelted pose
To the ever firm stories of that building —
That she would think of receiving
Her paycheck so she could
Go to K-Mart and have something.
But now years on top of each other,
Uncountable to her,
She continues guiding
The few of the masses of cars
That turn into the lot

Where to park: in winters
conscious of the visibility
Of her cold breathing,
And summers with the scents
Of greased telephone poles
And sights of light gleaming off
Car windows, she thinks
Of buying old junk from garage sales
For her yard sales, with the same prices,
So as to recall the sounds of human voices
Other than her own.

His job was a novitiate where there was no operator's manual
With which to have faith in, and no rules
But to move with the dustmop pushed before him
Along the empty corridor, and then down a staircase
Where he could descend to more passive depths in cleaning.

At home he would smell the odor of his bare feet coming to
    him;
Would see the blue under his toe nail that looked like marble;
And these would be dominant sensations
Though he would be vaguely aware of them.
Beneath his bended legs he would sweep his hand
To capture a fuller scent as his fingers would flick
His unshaven face. Then in his only room where the bare
    mattress
Was lain along with his leather jacket
And the dirty underwear cuddled around a clean toilet —
Where the Rosary hung on a wall
And the guitar leaned in a corner —
He would do his push-ups.

Most of those early mornings some train
Would pour its breath to the weeds
At the edge of the tracks, losing them
In sound and mist of a voice
Screaming out, alone,
Through the cold and the living.
His arms would tremble
With the body weakening, and then demobilized, to the floor
Before the count of fifty.
Through the fogged condensation
Of the upper corners to a window
He would glance up at the train —
Each car imagined as the girlfriend, Cindy,
Or the seminary, which he never

Grasped or rejected and so
They slipped away;
Or his mother, who with cancer
Began to close herself off to him —
Grasping one of those trains appearing at the time
With the familiarity of two strangers
Who recognized each other's desire to remain such.

ORACION A TRAVES DE GASSHOLE

(Patron Saint of Respiratory Therapy Workers)

Saturday. All the same:
A silvery grey
Thin and undistinguishable
From skies to parking lot
In exact shadow; and he finds his car.
The lid, laced in rust,
By the turn of the key,
Parts the grey as it pulls up;
The grocery bag is dropped into the hole;
And the hamburger, slaps down on the floor
Of the trunk as if a second slaughter,
Its grounded nerves convulsing it
A couple of inches nearer the oil stain.
That meat, in body, that last moment
After consciousness has severed itself;
Skin peeling under the fur, hidden,
But not from the last hot beams ahead
Of emerging dusk, becoming crisp
And then soaking up the hot blood, as the trachea,
With the last of the air drawing in,
Begins to fold its walls; and he could imagine it
Like he could imagine, from unexact memories,
The woman, last night
At the hospital, whom he began to like —
Her body pulling cell by cell
Apart before he had a chance
To finish the rescue with the hose

Descending the nostril as a rope,
And then flushing out mucus.
He gives the hamburger an air-born somersault to the bag
And closes the lid that is connected to the
Vague light bulb of the trunk.

20

The Gasshole's reflection on the trunk lid
Is lank and curved; the appearance of his face
With its facial tip of the nose and its greased
Separation of hair like a wet muskrat in a metallic reflection.
His face moving away, he sees an old Hispanic man
Who walks from the area of cars carrying two bags
Of groceries in an embrace that could be
For weighty children; he thinks "The senescent,
Carless, careless baws — turd! A campesino!;"
And he envisions himself as that: having to pull out the thorns
That pierce through his tennis shoes as he shovels
Scattered cacti leaves from out of the back
Of the pick-up to his animals;
And living in the dry ravine surrounded by houses made of
    wood
That
Had been patted loosely together like adobes, beside
The families of the kiln workers
Whom with him eat out Land's blessings
And piss and shit out onto her graces,
But himself happily not knowing the language of the Mexican
People . . . himself not wanting to know the language
Of any people that his sister, Cindy, and college pal,
Dave Broom-Up-The-Butt,
                    Echo.

He does not wish to think of them
Or the vaginas that are not his to put on
Or the illusive woman who would be sick with him
Like a child laying on the sofa in fever and hoping
That in the shadows on the wall and the
Passing sounds that are concentrated on her mind
One will bring deliverance — only placing the deliverance
On him and yet loving him for himself
Beyond that need. And while unlocking the door of his car

He feels that the recreation in life is also a routine:
A routine of sharing and parting,
And at the end one is grounded and tossed in
Before the validity of his own
Perceptions is resolved. But he is alive,
Now: and he will put away his groceries;
Read a chapter of his Biblia,
A cenotaph of the dead . . .
Maybe a verse; think of forgetting mass
And mailing in his tithing
And to veg' himself away a few hours
Before he would have another night
Of throats, lungs and
                    The air
                           Of the masses.

COME

(Camp Wonderland for the Retarded, Lake of the Ozarks)

Grabbing the already read letter,
Slipping out hot and wet
From the bare mattress —
Like Sweet Pea's turds
Right before
his psychomotor seizures,
Only without a softness to stub myself
Into — stiff and hard I drop
From the cold rim of the bunk
(Even if I awaken
The idiots below).
With non-syllables
And vowelessness
A pitch that is language enough
To keep this man, Jim,
From wherever
The unassimilated disappear
Howls "He does not want me here"
While its flesh of Jim beats the plastic urinal
On the walls barricading a pillowed head.
The joke is on him this time . . .
All over him for the next hours.

The letter's impression
Writes and rewrites in my mind:
Come, my sister calls to our father
Like Ronnie's suppositories butting back.
Only suppositories are meant to do so.
Come, she speaks to me,
And the shrink
Shall put in touch
All that he did to us.

23

Tripping over Keith's mattress
I step out in humid silence
And wipe my cheeks.
Two cabins, beside ours, simultaneously fry
Bugs in blue, electric lights.

Keith, a crippled rocking horse of autism,
Scrapes the feet of his vibrating body
To the bench where I sit.
Sit, Keith; go back to bed, Keith;
Go to the bathroom, Keith:
In this camp I shape the minutes of his life
To some acceptable pattern.
He rubs his hands together
As if trying to spark fire
For the inhabitants
Of his imaginary world.
Stop that, Keith, I say. Sit, Keith.
Keith sits: there is no coming out
For him after twenty years
This way,
Or perhaps for me.
The pale gas lamps
Are strewn around
A small area of limbs
In a corner of the sky —
All but patches are aflame
Like a roof of a tent around
The stakes, ready to break off
And fall.

Rock, Keith,
As the sun is stroked
So far into the lap of the night,
Suffocating and as good as gone.

The folding and unfolding
Of a crinkled letter into squares;
The imagining of the counselor
Of cabin four,
And what a pulse would have created
If her head had drowsed
To my hand on the back of her seat
On our way here;
The general silent howling of 'Come!' —
Similar thoughts are not his.
Keith does not cripple to this.
He has no sister that calls a stranger back
To erase and draw back
Them both.
He does not say 'Come!'
All hours.
He comes.

He must have thought
That there was some covenant of the old
That bound each to move around it
In a square orbit.
He was fifty now, so there
Must not have been any question:
Lessen the speed at the train tracks;
Stumble his car over their ribs;
Swerve closely to the drive
At a slower pace, and hope

That where men dodge the bumping
Of their tails from parks
For a private club,
That one would come
Out from the doors, partnerless.
If not, he would have
To go around the block
Another time
Like other old fags before —
The railway crippling with
Its iron in each return raising,
Cracking up from the skin of the street;
Limbs of that bar's tree
Waving down (some
To the windshield), warning.
Thoughts that the energy of youth
Had some pivotal focus
Made each imagined man to him
Like a lollipop,
But the parks would not do:

There the man with the smashed fender
Might be obligated to 69
A winner without a face —

A drag race ending in the winner's backseat, ·
And on his tools which would rib in.
And inside that bar where women snuggle
Away their faces in equality,
And where men rotate hips on the dance floor
Like an earth's axes . . . this would not do:
For there were no friends to affect
Mutually and faggishly in embraces;
And the young and sensitive
Were Oriental and fonder
Of the cigarettes
They put in their faces
And the beers that suddenly appeared
Before them. This would not do:
Mouth-hugging the earth
On its bulge of life
Or moving to songs
Where the dances never end.
He was an old fag and must retain
A square orbit.
It, at least,
Was a gentleman's right
And in accordance with the
Manner of the fags.
The block was long.
In the shadows and oblique actualities
He felt its length. His stomach tightened
In fear of the length.

No, the supremity of having been split off from
A larger entity by being spit out
From pussy lips while
Reeking pain and havoc
Like a living tongue pulled
From aperture and den
Is not sign enough
That he is meant
To be sustained as
An integral part of the world,
Unique and indispensable.
Thinking about how much longer
He will need to play out the day
That issue is not his, and never has been.
'The job was done'
He could say, later,
After the storm.
Hand-limp,
His broom dance-sweeps
Upended under an empty park bench —
Dirt caught under
The tongues of his feet —
So his paycheck
Will come in the mail
And become bank figures
He can suck from
To keep he and his woman
Housed and fed, and well enough
To legally rape each other in embraces,
Forgetful of their lives.

The man has a son,
And stands nights
Aching behind an assembly line,
Sleeping the days away

While his son goes to school.
The son thinks his father
Is thoughtless and dirty
And his mother a grease-bitch
For marrying him.
The son grows up
Between his college books,
And begins to put it together:
A society of men
Wanting to take a variety
Of stimulating produce —
Though some were more the makers
Than the takers;
The image of rightness
In a man putting his hormones
To the making of a company
In a family; a family
That needs a provider to survive;
A man honorable and trapped.

And there are nights
He awakens, gagging at the
Sudden thought of a man
Next to him
Who had engaged his body
In a lower form of sharing.
And he wonders if embracing a world
Of ideas can be done
When all things cannot be believed;
If humanism is
Energy vented
To avoid futility;
And what grossness
He would have to justify next —
All on those nights

When self-perspectives
Are swept under in change.

MAN OF COAL

You knew it was coming:
Twenty-three years and the mine
Would notice you one time,
Photo-copied.
A voice below bellows
Your name, Dave,
Into the settling air of coal-dust.

After you shut off the engines
And descend beneath the dragline's skeletal
Nose which canopys like a skyscraper on
Its side in mid-air
You confront a face
You cannot see in the descending sun. Shadow-still,
Enormous might engulfing over you
To the height of
The dragline's triple-tank wheels,
You see him —
The heels on his leather boots
Locked in the train-track grooves of dirt.

As he hands the notice to you
Its stiffness shakes
In your calloused hand.
You know that what is left of the day
Is becoming cold; and despite the smell
Of dirt there is a scent
Of watermelon in the damp air,
Though you do not know it as that smell
Or that there is a smell at all, really.
And yet a faintness of some half-knowledge
That touches its weight lightly in your mind,
Drags itself into places you cannot reach.

Pulling out of his shadow
You think of how you might hand
This sheet to your wife
Like a child presenting to his mother
An award from school:
Your wife screaming laughter of relief
As she hugs the paper to her breast;

Or how your strong hand might sweat
As you pick up the receiver of the ringing phone,
Expecting that after saying "hi"
That one of your college children's voices would end
The conversation there
For you to hand the vibrations
To your wife — but instead
That child
Congratulates you
For no longer destroying the land.

The noon hour whistle
Vibrates the walls
Of the hollow heavens
To the cab; the thermos-well
Of soup, sitting on your lap, you cannot see, but
You feel its stillness
Stagnating and absorbing
The contaminating minerals
Of the tin, walling in the contents;
And still you want to turn on the ignition
To finish out one more complete day
In the twenty-three years here
Of hard work.
The quandary then snaps, and you escape.

When out of the valley you enter the truck
And close the door —
The second time harder, and it latches.
You turn the key
And the truck bounces to the highway.
You stop at the sign;
Stop the motor while
Still on the dirt road;
But in the end turn left, again,
Home.

Mental Account, Some Day of Gorbechev, 1987

Another hour.
There is no circulation
Beneath the steering wheel for my feet.
Outside myself
There is the last of the sun at dusk
But like the conquering Hsuing-Nu
Pushing themselves beyond a
Great Wall and through an eternal
Gathering, it is hardly felt.
There is nothing great to trouble me
And nothing substantial descends on my senses,
Giving me thoughts other than the fact I'm thinking nothing:
Only
A flock of birds in the corner of my left eye
Blend down with the grey skies
As if the fence barricading
The farm land does not pertain to them;
Thoughts of the center line
And not going over it.
Days of Gorbechev, the radio speaks of,
But not his nights — where, one time
He may have smashed
A big, red cigarette in an ashtray
With an action stiff and slow;
And as he stood up the mattress of his bed may have
Raised to touch his rear, again,
Like a quick and soothing give-me-five handshake;
And opening a window of the embassy
To escape the stuffy dryness
Of electric heat in his suite,
He may have let the cool American air
Attack him with the smells and sights

Of its diplomatic car exhausts,
Grey and orange from street lamps
And store lights . . . and how
The nation breathed for once as it moved.

The third: road; cows, like islanders;
Multi-tinted bladed fields broken by acres
Of forests and pastures; a back-sun scene with
Car lights; a vision blurred and pebbled
Through the windshield —
A truck passes my pinto;
Muddy water slapping its face;
Its stick eyes smoothing it
To a duller complexion.
It isn't yet Christmas
And I am going home.
My parents one day drooped
In front of all, and were old —
We should be having much to say . . .
I, thinking like them, with
The mind of the world,
And us smiling unhappily
And speaking none of that:
But a lot will be said.
I am a bum.
One of their hearts shall give in
And their marriage will be a farce . . .
Even in car accidents the married
Die separately. And then the widowed
Mother, smoking the cigars of her husband,
And coughing them as the husband had done
But in the apartment of the son, might
Visit away her life: I would
Bring her there, thanking God for a reason

Not to try hiding all of me in some pussy
As in daylight the main part
Goes into underwear.

This is their town,
Far from trays with saucers
And plates and spoons and forks
(Sometimes hardened in scalloped potatoes
Or bent) and knives and glasses
(Glasses sometimes with folded bread inside) . . .
But forever coming down the belt for the
Dumping and washing . . . the trays that disappear
In a square hole and come out clean
Will continue regardless if I am there.
Men fuck virgins; a child-worker
Is born and all is holy.
There is nothing great to trouble me:
The rains that drop and drift next
To streets in gutters, take away
Smashed Pepsi cups and beer cans
Without intent, bound God knows where,
But out of sight.

MADDOG

Or Death to the Barbie-Dame Image

You said that it happened — that day you ran away
From a self you buried underneath the ice-packed snow,
All those cold years ago — when your last friend, then,
Had put an end to the Gabriele whom I've never known. This
Friend, like yourself a Barbie Dame, became totally lame and
Withdrew out the door when you needed more hands to keep
 your
Epileptic roommate
From smashing her head on the floor.

Gabriele, held together by the stitching of hate —
The plastic-eyed polar bear with the stiff arms
That the factory of the human race mutantly created —
This time it will be you who shall feel the wall of artificial
Fur ripped from its threads, and your stuffing falling out.
For a little maddog on top of four joints
Makes a person see the unsealed human fragments
That had been smoothed over in time
Like a million and some bone fractures
The milk of approval had swum into and covered over for looks.

For me fragmenting came yesterday when I saw a welcome mat
 iced
Over and yet I entered: your house was hot and your oven
Smelled of baking meatloaf though you had said that you could
Not be domesticated. And then I saw your bottle of wine
Standing at attention before two glasses. The pledge that
Bowing to anything or anyone was wrong . . . that people were
 only
Needed to gain the most bare of physiological and psychological
Needs (Pitstops to being human) — this was gone.
Gone with your hair brushed and your skin smelling of perfume
For some other man than me.

Come one Gabriele, the gal' that used to chew tobacco and spit
    it
Into an empty beer can . . . the gal' with the deep dark-ocean
Eyes . . . the maddog gal', grip that wine glass now.
For Gabriele, you smile at everyone with meaning.
You are as together as a feather when a hurricane is in town,
And when the hangover's over and your own insight has
    fragmented
You from a million pieces to a billion, my stiff polar bear arms
Shall poke and not embrace.

I sit back at this party I am hosting —
My back firmly pushing against the back of my chair,
And my head and eyes cocked.
You all are the performer this time . . .
And Gabriele, you are the main attraction,
Attracted, after this night, to the omni-present sense of your
Smashed self; and me — sensitive little me in no-man's land
Where no man wanted to grasp me from . . . and no
    woman —
Mended back together in thy survivalistic polar bear image.

BECKY'S DEMON

I
'Something happened.
I don't have those visions anymore.'
And you believe with a mind like Papa believed with
When I told him I could see things
Clearly before they actually were.

His back and forth pacing from those same two windows —
Which had been like a toy soldier powered on a human
        Battery,
With a three minute's stand at one, and then the next —
Suddenly stopped. For I was different. You annointed me
And cast me out. I was alone. You caused me to hide
        Beside
A pitchfork in the shadows of the corners of the barn.
Yes. Papa stopped. His eyes moved. I'd never seen his eyes
        Move
Before. They stared down at me. My child's eyes
Below — and he aimed his for them as a fisher for prey in clear
        Waters.
I backed up behind the pipe of the kitchen stove . . .
But with one stretch he reached his arm over
Like a bear's paw that in force comes down like a Redwood.

My knee aching as if broken, I crutched up
From the other side of the room, beside the door. . . .
Then, bending on my knees the next conscious second —
Feeling the blood of knee caps sticking to hay and dirt —
Seeing the sun poke like sticks through rafters and cobwebs —
Thinking I grabbed a hold on the sunlight which could
        Lift me
Up like a rope; but grasping the pitchfork —
Raising the pitchfork —
Pitching the pitchfork —

After hearing the creaking and scraping of the opening barn
   door
          Plowing
The top soil of the dry earth. Thinking: he would never kill
My shadowy corner.

II
And in this plush chair of the Bishop's office I sit a decade
And a half later — a Salem witch of the west explaining her
Dull, trembling self before three Mormon men bending above
          Me.
But you don't understand me, as if anyone ever has.
I had psychic abilities. But you don't want them, so they're
          Gone;
And I'm good. I no longer believe, Bish'y, that I saw Benson
          Dying
And yourself rising from his grave, standing above the
          Twelve.
But you're still scared of me. You only want to anoint me
And cast me out. You only want me to hide in a barn, and
          Belong to shadows.
You call my abilities a possession of a demon.

Papa doubted I could see; and you see me as perverted.
But you do see that I see . . .
That I have something with some power.
You and the missionaries lay your hands on me . . .
Me who left my Protestant roots so as to be rooted in your
          Family.
You put your cold hands on my forehead,
Trying to vacuum out my psychic abilities,
Which I tell you are no longer —
Trying to take away my saying that I'm okay . . .
I'm good. Speak to me. Don't cast me out and leave.

I can see you in those dry moments, then,
As clear as if I were there: staring at the cracks
Of the white ceiling above the bedpost, wondering if
You will slip down three flights to the outer darkness
Like your ex-Mormon roommate, here. Your visual mind,
Against your will, probably thinks about your squirm
That a few moments ago squirmed you of your juice,
Wiggled her skirt back on, resurfaced the lip-spit
Crackup in her concrete of make-up, and wordless,
Walked like a princess out the door.
    As the last of the ecstatic vibrations tides you in the rear
You arise from the raft of the mattress.
Then you cover up your nakedness,
And move to the light of the living room.

And then I actually see you, Don, in the hour that you had told
Me to step back in. You are bending over the end-table stained
In the blood of wine. Sunlight, stripped silver from the grey
Clouds, pours through the window to the table.
To your right a nine of swords card of a man pierced in the
Back gleams as it walls the card of your future lovers.
And the redness of **Doctrines and Covenants** to the far left of
That table also looks pure in the light.
    You do not see me. Your mind is racked in screwing the pack
For an answer. You turn another Tarot Card
In the order your destiny is to be read.

    Your sad eyes look up
And your languid voice says that you are late
For your meeting with the local Bishop . . .
A meeting to straighten up your fucking life.
I laugh! In bitterness that shakes my intestines, I laugh!
Another hillbilly man
Has lifted his head above the rest — a foot up from the jug —
And has blown his breath into the air

41

Which 'naps another young and fragmented one
To the call of being holy.
    But before you arise
You turn the gleaming card of number four —
Your eyes in a more motionless trance than before.

WHERE, OH WHERE, DID THE MALL-LADY GO?

They wanted her to drop her thoughts
As naturally as her underpants fell, after they were
Over the hips, so the steaming winds of her daily showers
Could clear her of encroaching stain
As she had been cleared away.

They were a function, ignorant of their thinking, charting
Charts. She felt she would have to ignore these doctors and
Nurses in the mental ward.
She would have to ignore the pacing patients
Asking cigarettes from her.
The hall was rectangular.
Everyone moved rectangularly.

She would go to dreams of past realities
Where she was watching the shoppers' reflections
As they passed mall's little fountains —
Different types of people-reflections but all silvery
In the still of the waters,
Happy and part of the lives of the mall.
She would imagine herself sitting on a metal bench —
Packages of her new clothing pulling on arms and chest
Like the recalling torpor that came more easily
To her lower legs; the weight of the mink that arched
Her aching shoulders more like a lady;
And a small sack of chocolate stars
Touching her upper neck —
Wondering what packages her fellow-creatures
Bought to be brought home and to whom
They brought them to.
And then, as the locks of solitude clicked in her consciousness,
Came the wondering of where, oh where,
Did the Mall-Lady go?

ESTIVATION

Weekends in Tranquility Park —
With the downtown buildings, hallways of giants clustered,
Exhaling the coolness echoed
From the rectangular mouths of doors
Opened and closed by cityers —
A coolness came over my thoughts
The way lack of wind contains
The hastening of Yosemite's flames.

There, diurnal and punctual, she crossed
That small area of grass, fountains, and cement,
Which were generally buffeted more fully by sun and adjacent
Sounds, moving the park more than Bush and Dukakis'
    presence.
"WALK" was always lit when la chica
Approached the street, carrying her library books.
When would she, artificial and pneumatic,
Who like Houston's miniature stop-lights
While going to work, veer my movement
To slide off a plane ticket and be led
Through and from burning Amazons
And green-house climactic changes —
Through wasted ozone and my own depleted life —
The breath of her mouth my only nourishment.

Masking tape
From hurricane threats
Remains at the edges of window panes;
Palm trees, below, are hybrid to cement;
Thuc Nguyen's business-report figures
Blend and bury themselves as distant sounds;
The staff meeting and this cigarette industry are gone.
Slid off a plane ticket caught in life's winds   restless
No friends for real   all wanting something from me

44

The outside world has nothing except life-ending amusements
    of
Sex to escape void   the dead have some solidity of truth
About what happens after life even if they are not aware of it,
And the rest breathe in fables   everything is surely unchanged
In Springfield, Mo., where I was raised, but none of it is mine
Nothing is ours — humanity drifts along and intersects briefly
In alliances   my friends are co-workers whom I must expire
    my
Life with civilly as we light cigarettes and bitch of no new
Raises

When would she pull on my arm
Tugging me thoroughly into breaking glass
To fall, putting me out violently,
When I can no longer dream.

Through the hazy waters
Of his hot bath, looking, he thought
That his woman's pubic hairs
Should naturally have come out
More permed like his,
Regardless of her color.

The door being shut and locked
With a rifle in front — still he heard
From the living room a forum of senators'
Televised voices discussing laws of limits
In openness and freedoms,
And ramifications. He did not understand —
As the mirrors steamed, dripped
Down from the air conditioning's touch, and resteamed
When it shut off;
And when he wondered what home owners
Had used the bathtub before
And what disease might be
Dropping from the cracks around the faucet — that
The fags would push down the American way of life.
He did not argue that if they were isolated
From the mainstream, their liquids might get off on any
    products
As they worked for the cost of their isolation
In, for example, a barren region of Texas;
and that the isolated would, by the testing of the
Virus, be proved witches
So there would not have to be witch hunts —
No, he just felt their destruction.

And he thought of his woman
In the bedroom, waiting, and became
Forgetful of anything
But the desire to have her.

They had that freedom. The American constitution
Said so — freedom to live and breathe
And fuck and fuck . . .
Fuck so hard that the penis would
Knive through the condom
And spray-paint the man's name
On the dull walls of the vagina.
They had that freedom — those unalienable rights —
Her to be banged and to squeal
To her friends that she was in love
And him to white pussy
And a gal that he could call his own . . .
His woman. And if the initial M got ready
To graffito-crawl his way out —
A problem for the rest of their years —
She could erase it, not remembering it
With any more significance than
Having clipped a broken end
Of a fingernail. She had that right.
Her man said so, and so said
The American constitution.

His shift in Toastmaster
Had for that day ended,
And so now he could rest in waters;
Focus on the bubbles that arose
When he farted; and let the memories
Of the entire day he released to rise and fall
Like the steam.
He would have to scrub himself
Good before going to his woman:
She understood wealth
With its charm of a cocaine high
But the composite smell of miscellaneous drugs
That he sold before each shift

Would lessen the good feelings that made
That understanding.

A Raphael in the Sandbox

First will be a billiard room,
But the balls' aims will collide and
Fall into forbidden pockets.
There is a boy in the sandbox.
He cannot see the persona of himself
That will be the man.

Then he will be along the cold and lifeless waters
At Virginia Beach, cognate
With the vanquished under the sunset
Or their emptiness that is vanquished
Like those multi-colored balls
On the pool table, in shallow knockings,
Fateless misdirections brought in clash,
Wars of void. He will see no seagulls

Swiping into their entities the digestive life-force
Of shallow, misguided fish.
On that day he will find himself
Nearly the only creature there.
His arms will cuddle each other
In rigidity; his stiff feet
Will staple down the sands and snow
With metallic movements.
To him the ocean will have stagnated in its vast depths.
Its body will not evaporate.
None of its water will be shared with the skies
For the giving to the earth.
No water will roll off soils and sands
And tactualate cartographic wanderings.
There will be no combining into soothing
Arms of rivers which eventually
Come back to impact the great captive
Body of ocean that makes the ecosystem
Reverable.

To himself he is a forever of
Space and substance unconnected
And unconnecting.

> There is a cricket in the sandbox,
> And a sandbox in the yard
> That is part of the township.
> The cricket senses the legs of boys
> Which are like four mountains
> Quaking around its world
> It chirps unafraid.

That morning will come, for the man he is to be,
At last in bliss. It will be a bliss where there is nothing to
Think
And where his wars of void fall in rhythm.
The doughnut-spins in his car on an icy parking lot,
After having driven from the beach, will
Ease the clasping presence of the memory of his friend . . .
Or what was
His friend . . . the artist who stepped onto sidewalks
That are assembly lines of iron people, unknowing and
    unfamiliar.
He will call for his playmate of twenty years after seeing him
Step from a taxi, but no return.
The joint like a great
Asteroid
Splitting the ocean gives tidal waves
Of circular rhythms
That further erase that clasp. He will rationalize that
It would all fade . . . everything in general.
Goal: only to remember the fact of hurting
And to reel it across
Like a civil war compacted in a phrase of microfilmed
Newspaper to some distant space never to drill trenches and to
Hide from

Death as the wars mutilate around him, never to remember
The feeling itself.

The child does not see the goal of his manhood.
The child does not see his manhood. It is somehow distant
    space.
His friend is there now. A cricket is there now:
It shall be incorporated into the whole.
It will be the equal who imagined
Will be the great one adding the tunnels
That connect the Spanish sand castles he and his friend have
Built. He thinks that all three will go to visit
The real ones sometime.

When I am at a dead-lock
In your rear and the
Language of my body
Will not come from
The third element of the soul,
What am I to say? —
"'ALL BUT ONE DEAD:
Mexican immigrants celebrating the
Stowing away on a 120 degree boxcar
With urine in their stomachs,
Acknowledging capitalistic thirsts . . .
Sigue sobre pagina" . . .
Double hubble
The peso is in trouble
And to Mars
America plans
Jumping over the moon,
And all this has disturbed me!"

The night is full of impulses
To live and to run and seep heavily
Into its dark robes of
Silence and morbid rightness;
And as I, again, try to thrust on dryly —
A log without a river traveling it
To the product of lumber —
And hope to create love in
The smackings of night,
Like anyone else, I know that soon
I am to apologize for lack
Of an ejaculation,
And will promise to have a counselor
Tame me to the exclusion of
All but work and lust.

Sounds of people
Kicking around the
Night of early morning
Beneath my lover's window;
And I withdraw under the sheet,
Lying flat with the dead moonlight.

Taking the boat
Two hundred miles
With her Ozark-loving husband
Not having the key
And why I don't use
The hair masque I
Had bought from her
The last time
So she'd stop asking me
Why I don't use that
Conditioner this time
I say "Yes, Honey"
Though her lips, in the mirror,
Are still goin'
And another shampoo is
Ground harder in the scalp. My hair shall be chopped
Off another two inches more than what I had asked her to do.

In a room of old women, like me,
Who let the buzz of dryers
And loud beautician speakers
Keep their minds active from remembering,
My bored and wayward eyes
See in the mirror
(Now seated in a once empty chair
Next to mine) a young one:
Her fidgeting body willfully captivated;
Hair held high and hostage;
Curlers stiffly tightened;
Bulges diluvial by Cylinderic Bottle
Held ungodly above her head
And squeezed by gentle but firm hands
Of a male beautician —
And I remember that the noxious liquid
Dribbles under Cotton Crowns

Around one's head
As the eyes water from the sting.
Somehow I want to warn her
Though she may be a stranger
To be whitewashed
In a man's liquids
And the click-of-the-heels logic
Of women, as if
One's whole damaged life
Can be bounced from a mirror
In and to all women
Like an SOS.

It was as if certain people came in. Those disliked were
Disregarded and the rest kind of circled in and out but at the
Time in and a small period out were associated with and
Considered part of that person's reality by himself
The way a cat brushes against certain familiarities
Agreeable enough as it goes for its meal, and so I befriended
Places.

Saltillo in Mexican mountains when the land shivers in shadow
And the sun stretches through the air and beyond it
With an intent to overpower what is closer to man —
The River-Walk and the Alamo and between both where
A Philipino in green shorts eats the grass where
Sidewalk and road intersect. There is a city where I
Thought I could find myself less lonely,
And I have returned home. Snow embraces Springfield's earth
To its death.
Under the sounds of the rolling drips of water in the gutter
I am frozen, though fingers tearing apart the wet leaves
I had pulled off from a tree, wishing they had been
Dry to grind and become the physical appearance of wind.
Cracked and peeled back from a boot a portion
Of the snow is removed but refreezes more heavily
On one area of the dead. I stand as an outsider
Imagining myself to allow a job section of today's newspaper
To become the thoughts that clash along in the mind of the
    wind.
I need money but cannot find anything worth doing.
To change from a person to a commercial function to eat . . .
This . . .

This day I shall sleep away
As the night. In Springfield, Mo.
The Great God may also await for his eviction.
200 Indians in Houston bow down to Krishna as the gates men
    lock
Around him are opened. But in Springfield he probably awaits,
His red-sock feet on his sofa
As the furnace blows
The Soviet flag on the wall before his feet.
His walls may have many flags,
And his mind thoughts of glasnost and communism
    intermixed . . .
Impractical thoughts he must not sacrifice so
                        that he could exist together
                        more easily with the community
                        of the dead,
                                unalone.

THE PHILOSOPHY OF RITA AND HERB

Staring fixed at the rows
Of flowered
Wallpaper a pale-grey
In the dark efficiency —
The three walls still absent
To her consciousness
As a shadow of silver lightning
Fades the greyness
Of one portion in her view —
The "schizophrenic" lifts
Up a cigarette hidden behind
An ashtray and the flat ground
Of ashes on the table, which
Skid and resurface with her
Hot breathing. She thinks they are
Continents drifting, and herself
Upon them.
From feeling stiff and pushed under —
Numb to the point of a corpse —
With insecurity enough not to remember,
Even, her ABC's, Rita runs into the night
Where outside of a window
She blesses the workers making
Colonial bread.

An old man in a cowboy hat, Herb,
Is saddled on the wooden railing of a porch
To an apartment complex: seated there beside a remembrance
Of a young woman like Rita.
And in the spitting fumes; bad-muffler sounds;
The rocking phallicism in radio music of passing cars,
He feels he has to move or die
And gets down
To his pickup.

And Rita, upon dawn and upon the end of rain,
Walks the streets again after tiring,
Ready to go back and confront the curfew-conscious
Group home, and the "zero" on her record full of
Zeros. She worries about carrying in her womb
A mini-Herb with scabs of grey hair
And little pot-holes in his tiny face,
Though she is still a virgin.

Aten,
Where it is throned
On the television
Beneath the window,
Sees above and below
And says nothing:
It enjoys the woman secretary
And the road constructor
Who from opposite shifts of the sun
Come to it, the cat;
Follow the roaming in its mansion;
Pensively laugh as it clings to
Hundred dollar drapes;
Feed it holiday popcorn
On the throne;
And close the drapes
That the cat, Aten, had opened
By its tugging,
And will open again:
Opening below
  Where the woman, statue of her liberty
  Wedged in a mud layered hill of snow ankle-thrusts
  The tilt of her body after a moment of standing still:
  Face looking in the trash receptacle that her flabby
  Breasts rest on the rim of and point toward; head bowed
  To the tin; And mind distinguishing between good and
  Bad trash. Her hands raise from the snow-blended
   mixture
  To push back the hair that was intimate with trash.
  She raises her head and glances up at the sky that she
   had
  Noticed a few seconds earlier; and wonders of the person
  Who could throw away a nightgown and wilted plants,
   dented
  But unopened cat food, and scattered baby pictures —

but the
Cold wind pushes further into her rashed cheeks; and
    she
Drops the gown before she can visualize the woman's
Possible image. She digs further and . . .

And opening Above where
Two crossing jet
Had each made an element
Of a cross in the skies —
A third, now, and the
Heavens appear to play
Tick-tack-toe with their bad arts,
Or do not know how to push out caulk neatly
When hoping to seal out the heavens.

Afferent, the city bus cramps to the curb and brakes through
Solipsistic muteness with an exhaltation startled and choking.
[People are play-things in one's reality! One must look
Into other eyes or he'll be reminded that he is a user too]
As the sun-god, Aten, blazes upon the terminal's
Scraped concrete — its graven image —
Making the place an Amarna,
The shelved rows of the poor men
Hear the sound humbly grazing
Through whispered reverence over
The glass-speckled pavement
In a gradual dying echo.
A cigarette succumbs to the voice as
Carrion brought to life; all the tattered people awaken;
And a man spits toward the tire of the bus,
Bus misses.
[Religion is a lie! Everything is a lie!]
And as he watches his own spit vanish
From the hard crest of the world,
And silently scrapes his lunch pail against
A corner of a metallic bench as if expecting the pale to
    bleed . . .
And hoping it would bleed . . . he tries to remember the angles
He and his wife stood to project
The intermingled shadows that both
Had labled as their marriage.
[Marriage, that sanctified legal rape, fosters
The child-man to be a destined societal function
As he grows up in the family unit]

He enters the second bus:
Its coolness sedating the skin that
Overlaps his troubled mind.
His thoughts pull together
Like the light, cool flow of the air conditioning.

He feels a little pacified.
[Come to thyself, human, the refuge from lies!]
He knows the shadow's intangible depth:
Its vastness having overpowered him these months
Until he could not reach the logic that told him
To find himself outside its barriers.
As he stares out of the window
He wonders why she has left.
How could she have left without indication
When he has remained angled toward work
So that he and his wife can stay alive?
In the bus window he sees his diaphanous face — the windows
Of the Hilton, where he has a job in maintenance,
Piercing solidly through its head. He rings the bell.
The idea of her not home, and legally annulled
From his life — her small crotch not tightened to his desperate
Thrusts — makes him feel sick. He gets down from the bus.
He goes to work. He suddenly knows that he is not in love.